Following
the Light

New and Selected Poems
by Kevin Bezner

Also by Kevin Bezner

Poetry
About Water (1993)
In the City of Troy (1994)
The Tools of Ignorance (1997)
Wherever (1999)
Particularities (2000)
The Hungry Walker (2001)

Edited by Kevin Bezner
The Wilderness of Vision: On the Poetry of John Haines,
with Kevin Walzer (1996)
The Way Home: On the Poetry of Colette Inez (2003)

Following the Light
Copyright © 2014 by Kevin Bezner

Published by Kaufmann Publishing

ISBN 978-0-9905329-2-7 (hardcover)

Everlasting Memory

Mary Rita Sullivan Bezner
September 20, 1923–June 23, 2013

Following the Light

CONTENTS

PREFACE

The poems collected here are the result of reflection that at first resembled and then later became a form of meditation and prayer. For the most part, they capture moments during which I felt either in the experience or in the writing a presence I now know was God.

I was far from God when I began writing poetry. I had taken a long and circuitous path through journalistic and academic worlds that had led me from a lack of interest in the Catholic faith of my childhood and youth to agnosticism and finally atheism. Through a variety of writers I admired, I gradually found my way to poetry, nature, and Buddhist spirituality, which taught me how to see and experience the world around me. The more I came to experience the natural world, the more I was drawn to God and Jesus Christ.

I understand now that all along I was seeking God in the beauty of art and the world, and that poetry and nature were just two of the instruments he used to soften my hard heart. Another instrument was Pope John Paul II. One early morning when everyone in the house was asleep and I could hide what I was doing, I turned on the television, flipped through the channels, and found myself absorbed by a show on EWTN. The program I watched showed Pope John Paul II in prayer. Even through the filter of a television screen I knew that I was witnessing great holiness and that he was in the presence of something I did not understand but desperately needed to know. Although I wandered several more years, I eventually experienced for myself the power of true prayer.

Part of my journey to the light of Jesus Christ is recorded in these poems. While they are far from the brilliance of the writings of St. Paul, St. Augustine, and Dante, and they are not always specifically Catholic or Christian, they emerge out of my relationship with those places where we often encounter God, and where God the Father, the Son, and the Holy Spirit waited for me—in the beauty of the natural world he created and in daily life.

Charlotte, N.C.

Solemnity of the Annunciation
March 2010

Holy Hieromartyr Eusebios, Bishop of Samosata
June 22, 2013

Genesis 1:3-4

And God said, "Let there be light"; and there was light. And God saw that the light was good; and God separated the light from the darkness.

Psalm 36

For with you is the fountain of life; in your light do we see light.

Daniel 3:52

Let the earth bless the Lord; let it sing praise to him and highly exalt him for ever.

John 1:9

The true light that enlightens every man was coming into the world.

Ephesians 5:14

Therefore it is said, "Awake, O sleeper, and arise from the dead, and Christ shall give you light."

From About Water

(1993)

The Earth Does Not Need Us

Light of
yellowed

maples all down
the street. Old

earth, what use
words.

This is
your say, this

warm color,
this warm light in

cold
autumn.

When Evening Comes, Winter

The light, the sun
beginning

its old descent
in the cold gray and blue sky with

a trail of red, enters
through the thin

curtains, the room
illuminated.

Marsh

The air is so heavy with it,
you can feel the ink,

the blue of the paper mill's
ink. And yet

warblers skitter yellow
through palms, and great white

herons, pelicans, egrets fly low over
greening pastures.

Houses, Winter Morning

Always the same light from farmhouse windows,
the same light from the red saltbox behind maples,
now only gray lines against black sky, lines

the birds have left, the same light from the white
cottage on the edge of the cornfield, furrows
and stalks still visible in new snow.

Farm

Up the gravel
road past

the decaying barn the farmer
uses as a blind

to shoot
the crows that eat

his corn, the house
fading into

a stand of trees
opening into

meadow
and woods

and undergrowth.

Field

By the red barn, where
a horse nips another horse,

farmers, sweat wetting their faces,
look over the field, seventeen
bales of hay spread out below

the ditch, the summer wildflowers,
mostly purple, in a jagged line.

Field, Late Winter

In late winter, wildflowers and bales of hay,
but this is March, weeks before spring,
and now four wide stacks of graying branches,

a line of eight sheep, a cluster of four horses
in the grass, grazing, the barn and the house,
in wonderful symmetry, each on its own rise.

From The Tools
of Ignorance

(1997)

Following the Light

To Have Knowledge

Peel your body down
to the bone. Grind

the bone down
to a fine dust.

Now you're left
with the nothingness

we call self,
which is air, but isn't air.

God Explains Earth to His Angels

They would watch the colors of the sun, birds
all around them, animals and insects
of all kinds. They would watch the stars
and when they came out they would sit
with them for hours. Then

they began to make things.
They began to clear the land,
the green earth, the grasses, the trees.
They forgot about the sun, the stars,
and thought only of what their work

could bring. The animals
and the birds left them. The insects
became angry. I asked about this.
They cleared more trees.
They said leave, old man, go away.

A Bagful of Fish

I find a green plastic garbage bag in sea oats,
open it, and lay it in the water like a net.
My bag fills, the fish are so plentiful.
It's too heavy for me to lift.

I drag the bag to the lodge where it breaks.
I stuff back in the fish trying to escape.
My hands bleed.

I think I have salmon, but the fish are flat,
like none I've ever seen.
A fisherman laughs, says they're garbage.

The bag breaks again.
The fish snap at my ankles like small dogs.

Near Henry's Lake, in August

In the yellowed valley that will give way to green,
marshes, Montana, two

grazing sandhill cranes,
then seven more, then two, lightning

over the mountain, snow
flurrying,

the highest peak
clouds,

and ascending dramatic as the lightning,
this change in weather, twisting

like the dust in Nevada scrub
miles back where

the only shade
is cloud,

companions to the cranes, seven
ravens.

Grasshoppers, Summer

I have not seen them since I was a boy reaching
into high dried grasses

to cup them in my hands then
watch them jump. And

here they are on
the brown fence in the back yard
having leaped

out of the way when I bowed to look at
newly bloomed wildflowers.

Three, still.

I bend to one
and say, looking into

its left black unblinking
eye,

"So good to see you here. Eat
all you like, but
leave some

for the bees,
for the moths,
and for those like me—

we also come
to feed."

Vulture

Gravel kicks off
the tires, dust

rises from
the road. A vulture,

wings
wide as a lane, lifts

into trees and
leaves behind

the carcass
of a raccoon. High

over pines, it rides
the thermal, watchful

like Brueghel's magpie perched
on the gallows.

Birds

All day they
call out, not

for us, not
to us, but more

like the old sweeping
their walks, who

unaware of the man
passing

sing only for
themselves.

The Sparrow

The sparrow hits the windshield.
It falls onto the hood of his car.
He picks up the dead bird.
He puts it in the glove compartment.

After awhile, he forgets it's there.
Some time passes.
The bird's feathers fall off.
Its skin dries from the bone.

One day the man reaches for a map.
He finds bones stacked
like gray branches in a field
ready for burning.

Travel

How little we
actually

need. What
fits in a
bag.

How good to see
the herd of

goats,
wandering.

Leaf

Two days now I've seen it stopped
by the long left spinning of some spider
that has made its climb into the sweetgum
to build its web elsewhere. Twice

I've seen the morning light give it
a cast of yellow through a haze
of dust. And once, in the dark, I ran my
hand beneath it, curious whether

the spider had moved from ground to tree.
But there was nothing below the leaf,
which hangs suspended like a worm in spring

crawling through air up into the tree,
climbing from its one journey to earth,
as if it could make a path back to itself.

About Water

I stood on rocks looking
across water through salt haze, salt
staining my shoes. I look
for eels in the water, horseshoe
crabs in the grass. Nearby

is a cottage. A woman
who has lost her husband sits
on the porch and watches
me discover something

in the grass, in the water
that comes up from the bay to fill
the river and the marshes, in the salt,
and in her own content eyes.

I will never actually leave
these rocks or water in gray
New England, darkness coming on.

It is houses we want in loneliness.
The larger the house, the smaller the heart.

I would watch the houses of Newport longing
for their protective marble and stone,
cold and damp as they are.

But then I remembered, and I would sit alone
between the crevices of great stones
facing the sea and the sea,
great well, took my loneliness.

When I lost the sea I lost my way.
And I became like fire on the plains.

One night I woke to the sound of water
and I opened my eyes to salt haze.
And through the phosphorescence I saw

a boy sitting on rocks
under pines in deep woods
in his eyes the eyes of deer keeping
him in sight as he followed their movements
through meadow to stream.

And I woke to the cool dry air through trees,
the sound of water over rocks,
and the tongue of deer on my face.

The Pond: Fourteen Images

1.

Caterpillars
in silk
nests, birds sing

everywhere, drone
of wasps
and bees. Quick

smooth black
flies

land in mud.

2.

Cut, dragged
stacked high, branches

rise
from the black

mud. Bramble,
fallen tree,

solitary sparrow
sings, cardinals,

finches only
color.

3.

Dam of reeds
branches, and mud.

Long line of dead
trees. Ridge of

debris. Stream into
deep gorge.

4.

Hepatica grows
in protected

places,
and here

it is open, near
the road, not

protected
at all.

5.

High
in the red

oak, above the leaf
covered path,

the over flowing
creek, the cardinals

who fly low
into thickets—

the nest,
abandoned.

6.

The ground
moves. Spiders.

Numerous
black

spiders, white
marks on backs,

and one
bright orange

bug the size
of a pen's tip.

7.

The water collects
debris. Mud,

branches, algae:
The fallen tree, bark gone,
wood smooth, roots

still in one
bank.

8.

Thick along
the ridge, under

trees, broken
limbs, in grasses

above the stream
deep green from

weeks of rain,
Blue Woodland Phlox—

Phlox, to the Greeks
flame. So

blue
flame.

9.

Turtle leans
against dry

grass, pulls tight
into shell.

Fallen tree over
path, ground wet

near crimson sumac high
as my eyes.

Stopped, too,
wings still,

the red
dragonfly.

10.

Two crows wing
modestly

toward the next
ridge over

trees cased in
ice, one

a perch for
six fat

waxwings.

11.

Two jays tangle wings
against wings.

A doe kicks wildly
through leaves.

12.

Two sparrows, low
over thicket.

Hawk, low over
pines.

Buzzing
chickadees.

13.

Wind bends
browned reeds, dry
sumac. Chickadees

in the pines above
chatter. You
don't belong here

they seem to say
with the Canada goose who
strains on the water

to get a look, then,
slowly, arcs

to the opposite
bank.

14.

Woodpecker COOK;
COOK;

Cook; cook. How
far?

From Wherever

(1999)

Starlings Gather, Morning

Confused chatter falls
from the willow oaks with
acorns,

until dozens of starlings,
stark angles in steep climb, define
the trees—

which have emerged,
like the birds,
suddenly,

with still deep green leaves
and yellowed
leaves,

out of the dark and into
the soft early morning gray
light.

Pain

Pain burns, erupts
flows, and amasses,

floods the miles of a life

with ridged black basalt swirls, or
bone-colored glass-like spheres.

The igneous cruel,
the dull sleepwalkers—

formed by pain.

In one form
basalt congeals above

and beneath
the earth.

In another it pushes at the mountain's edge,
hangs suspended until
weather erodes its grip,

and it falls
and it crumbles.

A human life shaped by pain
must have within it
another life

to weather after
the weather of life
the life engraved.

Far

The bus takes me far
from where I want to go

The car my mother drove in '59
keeps passing by

I watch through the reflection
of the sleeping woman

I see in the fins
I thought were ugly

a certain beauty and wonder
how I missed it

After My Father's Death

I am driving with my father.
I don't know where we're going. Past

salt marshes, up the road that overlooks
the long river moving slowly in its winding way,

we move toward mountains I see in the distance
and I tell my father how great they are.

He smiles and tells me "just wait."
And while I remain in dream I am startled awake.

I want to say, "You died in May.
I saw you in the mirror in June."

But I say nothing.
I let my father drive,

looking out windows, feeling his presence,
moving toward mountains.

And Then

I often walk
disappointed

and then I'll walk
up the red brick steps

late afternoon sun
hazy through

trees rows of
yellow pink

purple flowers
birds feeding

and I stop there,
stand there

completely there.

Waiting

For thousands of years
I did not exist

Maybe I was lying
like a bear in deep snow

or like a flower bulb buried
in deep earth

waiting for the spring
that would be my life

April Night, Eclipse

Earlier the moon was
half earth's shadow

Now it's full with
a reddish ring

I stand beneath
the budding oaks

the leafing maples
breathing summer

Courtyard

Through the haze beyond
the trees the ragged
serpentine roils
of the mountains emerge

and the bowl brings you
back to the courtyard
the brick patio merging
with the wrought iron tables

chairs the aluminum pinwheel-
like sculpture against
the stucco building scooping
air like water

Chimney

Out of the slate
roof, two

pigeons on the next roof top
one house

over, the red
brick chimney, blue

sky in relief, the full
leafed tree in

the foreground, Blake's
evanescent soot-stained

boys, the calm,
the effulgence.

Tea and Snow

Today
the first snow

in three years
although only

flurries at
the moment

I have been leaving
under the trees and

the shrubs in
the backyard

the green tea leaves
I have used

I hope
there is enough

left in them
to produce

on this cold day
a cup of tea

for each
so that we might drink

together tea
and snow

To Think of Akira Kurosawa's *Dreams* One Morning Driving to Work

On the already busy
street

full moon
at dawn

pickup trucks and cars
pass me

by stirring white
Styrofoam

chips that swirl
in the draw

From long cut
peach trees

no petals
will fall

Place

A glimpse this
recollection of

sitting on a park
bench late

summer reading
a novel by a Boston
writer and

down below

through the trees
the river moving

toward the bay
on the other
side the town

left behind but not
in memory

which
always seeks in

every other

place the rocks
always the rocks

and the cold
water

Solstice, Morning

The moon almost
full a violin

from the next
room I look

through the slatted
blinds at

the moon high

over and between
the silver maple

the pin
oak only this

light in

the beautiful
dark

Max the cat stretched out
beside me

almost a bottle
of wine
tonight

The tree in the front
room furniture

rearranged

I am happy the Romans
worshipped
the sun

at December's
end

I am happy
for the sound

of the violin in

the beautiful
dark

I am happy for
the moon

Following the Light

Up

Up for
another

cup of
tea

snow
again Soon

the water boils
the steam

rises the snow
stops

falling only
the dirt

beneath
the two

pin oaks and
the cupped leaves

of the ground
ivy finely

beaded
white

Prayer

All steps,
all moves,

each spoon lifted
to the mouth,

every said word,
all thought.

Reading Jotei

Up late, sleepless
again, the old worry
that I've lived too many places
and so have missed my life,

I read poems by Jotei,
a poor poet and painter,
a wanderer and an unknown,
and I think how good it would be
to sit up with him

in the summer heat
no breeze but the words
from our mouths out talking
even the noisy crickets
who'll wake me
at dawn.

Reading Lu Yu

I am restless,
so I turn to my bookshelf.
I find an old companion,
Rexroth's Chinese poems.

I read how Lu Yu one dawn
hundreds of years ago
went to his shelf for books by writers
even longer dead.

Through Lu Yu I see
how the body cannot hold us.
We overflow it every day,
and while some like Lu Yu find a new container,
even then they are not contained.

Tea

Language, skin,
eyes, mind, voice—

why define yourself
this way.

Why should I say
I am Celtic and Slavic

but born in these forsaken
United States, away

from the lands
of my ancestors.
They are with me now

as I bend to hear
the voice of Bodhidharma
who has come to China from India,

while I sip the tea
of Soshitsu Sen XV,

or walk from the village
to the mountain
in Shih T'ao's painting.

Following the Light

I might as well be
Chinese or Japanese.

I might as well be
Lafcadio Hearn, who is and might be
my ancestor.

So even though it is cold
walk with me now.

When we are finished,
I will make you tea.

Wherever

I have lived many
places. Not one
I call home.

Like a turtle, I carry
hot wet air,
and cold dry air,

leafless trees in mist,
a mountain in endless
shades of light.

Always with me.
No burden.

From The Hungry Walker

(2001)

Somewhere

Mostly I would like to
disappear

one day here
the next day living

somewhere
like Dickinson I think

writing unknown in some
cool white room

windows on the sun
the rain

words
like weather

Thinking of Nina Cassian's Poem, "Couples"

What of the one
who loves

but isn't
loved except

as a pet to walk
an impressive toy

to bring out

always full
of desire always

looking

the hungry walker
passing by

the restaurant's
window

the haggard
unsettling face

The New Saint Joseph
Children's Missal

Open the cover and you see
a perfect Jesus on the cross,
perfect green trees, the blue hill,
the city in the background.

Blood has drained from his head to his feet.
His blood has stained the cross.
His bowed head rests on his right shoulder,
his halo colored red.
Still, he is beautiful.

Kneel before Jesus who is gentle.
Ask him to make you strong.
You must be sorry for your sins,
ask for the strength not to sin again.

You are sad because you know he has suffered,
sad because you know how his hands
and feet and bones were pierced.

My mother gave me this missal May 7, 1961,
the day of St. Stanislaus,
Bishop of Cracow, and martyr
killed by King Boleshaw the Second

Following the Light

for criticizing his life,
the patron saint of Poles,
saint from the city near the farm
where my father's mother was born.
Six days later I received my First Holy Communion,
the day of St. Robert Bellarmine, Bishop, confessor,
doctor of the Church, a writer.
In 1962, I was confirmed.
It is May 10, 1999, as I write,
thirty-seven years later.
Still, I love this Jesus, this Church,
holy water, incense, dark churches, Latin, the Pope.
Once a Catholic, always a Catholic.

I am the prodigal son.
I am the banished son.
I have left the paradise of childhood and the Church.
I have left myself.

The preachers push you away
with their hollow talk of a personal God,
their certainty, their politics.
What do they really know
but a shadow of the truth, the dust
and not what the rider on the horse knows.

Where are the churches of my youth?

I want to go back to St. Joseph's in Fall River,
back to the white clapboard St. Thomas More
    in Somerset,
back to St. Valentine's and Our Lady of
    Perpetual Help in Buffalo,
back to St. Mary's in Alexandria.

I once read this missal every day.
I have saved it through years of moving.

I have prayed for the living,
for the dead in purgatory,
prayed for those who hated me,
prayed for the enemies of the United States,
prayed to be saved from the bombs.

I believed the Lord would one day come,
that only he knew when the world would end.
I was not wicked, but I feared this end in fire.

I took solace in these words, these pictures,
the yellow light surrounding
Mary, Joseph, and the Child.
Mary's blue dress and habit.
The name of Jesus embossed on the sun.
Child Jesus preaching in the temple.
Jesus with the centurion.
Jesus calming the sea.

Jesus rejecting the most hideous devil,
the one with the odd shaped wings that look
    like fins,
the green skin of a frog,
the beautiful loaves and the mountains
    in the background.
Thomas with his hand in the wound.
Jesus with the lost sheep tangled in vines
    a hawk overhead.
Jesus at the last judgment encircled by angels,
his cross the brightest light.

Listening to Music, Watching Gray Sky

A ballad
naturally

sad

the knowing voice
of the singer

a few

words that hold

still before
falling

the voice the
words

clinging to
air

the wind
outside moving

Following the Light

branches

one white petal not
miraculous dozens

falling from
somewhere it

seemingly
can't

maybe only
a leaf reflecting the

white light through
clouds

Stones

I have known
happiness

holding in my
palms stones

I knew I must
leave

wherever
I found them

Rock

I am a rock
in a mountain

stream the cold
water cleanses

After Rain

The rain finally
stopped

the creek runs wild
white over riffles

as if this were water
where trout could hide

Geese float in streams
a week ago grass

These streams come and go
go where streams go

Wind through the trees
twigs and green leaves fall

The blue heron is gone
but perched in gray trees

above the muddied
beaver pond

two white herons
bright against all the gray

Following the Light

New Poems

Following the Light

Storm

Oaks bend in rising wind,
branches scratch at windows.

The insistent screech,
the thundering hail.

But we have no trees
that can reach our windows.

And there is no wind,
no crack of falling ice.

The air is thick
with hundreds of acorns,

the treetops heavy
with cacophonous birds.

Winter Nights

Falling snow, a whisper,
calling me into the quiet dark,
I don't know what I want

or why I walk past fields and courts,
past houses of friends I once knew,
along the river with its crust of ice.

I walk the snow hushed streets
wearing my uneasiness
like a threadbare coat.

Prayer for the Wounded

She feels it in the arm scarred in dream,
the clamped trap that stopped her breath.

The light in her eyes is gone.
They sweep the room as she rises.

If only she could shake it off,
like rain from her coat.

If only she could taste his kiss, feel
his gentle hands washing her wounds.

Demon

I was not human then.
I was not even bird or animal,
although I resembled wolf
with the timid heart of deer.

I was more ghost than corporeal,
yet dependent on sickening flesh.
Some called me demon. I meant no harm.
Still, I descended from nothing

to calmly take the lives of the unaware.
I followed nothing but desire,
seeking prey with large round eyes
bright as diamonds, treacherous as black ice.

Crossroads

"You're sad again," my old self says.
Today he's eight. He's just come in

from the old orchard, face red
with the breath of cold.

"I was reading about Hercules," I say.
"He was at a crossroads

and was asked to choose between virtue
      and pleasure."
"You found pleasure more appealing?" he says.

"I was sorry to realize that no matter which
      I've chosen,
neither has brought me happiness," I say.

"Pleasure can lead to virtue," he says.
"I'm virtuous now, but I'm not happy," I say.

"Let's walk in the orchard," he says.

Hiking With My Old Self

I'm out on a hike with my old self.
I've never seen him happier. He hikes ahead,
circles back. Then, he disappears.

I don't mind. I listen to the chickadees
and the breeze through the pines,
my feet crunching leaves on the trail.

Two hours pass,
and I come around a bend to a grove,
the ground thick with pine needles.

And there's my old self,
sitting with a bottle of wine between his legs,
bread and cheese spread out on his knapsack.

"You're slower than you used to be," he says.
"I've got ten years on you," I say.
"And you're used to hiking the Bitterroots."

"Have some wine," he says.
He takes out a worn copy of Rexroth's
Chinese poems.
"Let me read to you awhile," he says.

I sip the wine, eat the bread and cheese,
and listen to my old self read Tu Fu,
thousands of miles from home.

Snares

He's still a child,
Yet he teaches his elders.
At his age, I was a fool
Caught in the snares

Of popular music,
One day seeking the holy,
The next day the profane.
I took the wrong path

To unbroken years
Of misery, confusion,
Uncertainty and wayward
Disordered thinking.

I hungered for silliness,
Guitars and drums, love songs,
And street fighting anthems
That drowned out the truth.

Suddenly

Upside down
my heart drums.

Look, how calm
the trees.

Easter Lilies

Rising out of the loam
the white trumpets blare,

lifting you into
the joyous light.

Lilacs in Bloom

Jesus has fallen.
He is on his knees
looking up the road
in front of him, the cross
too heavy to lift.

I am watching.
The yellow cat sits
on the roof of the black car.
The black cat sits in the grass.

I am walking
with heavy steps.
I am thirsty.

After days of rain
I want to know the joy
of this cool sun filled dusk,
but I keep seeing Jesus
under the weight
of his heavy cross.

The cars and trucks
wind up the hill.
Someone plays a flute
in the valley below. It sounds

Japanese, bamboo.
Clouds cross green mountains
bright in blue sky.

I stop to look at the lilacs in bloom
along the unpainted picket fence.
My eyes fill with color,
my nostrils with fragrance,
my ears with the buzz of bees.
I am walking.
Jesus is in the garden.
His weathered finger
points to his heart.

Retreat, July

The covered boat drifts
on the calm gray lake.

Buzzing insects
birds and planes

join in lazy
summer song.

Jesus stands in the shade
of the lone leafy tree

facing the empty
winding road.

His arms are open,
his heart aflame.

Bread of Life

I.

I was with them,
the crowd by the sea
that questioned the Rabbi.
We wanted to know
how we could do the work of God,
how we could become
his true children.
The Rabbi said God wanted
only for us to believe
in the one he had sent,
the Rabbi standing before us.
I wanted to know
why God would send this man to us
in this very moment,
to be among us, to walk
the same ground we walked,
to drink and eat as we drank and ate.
If he had been sent,
then let him show us a sign.
But he would show us no sign.
I felt confused in his presence.
Some were laughing. Some were angry.
But he was like a mountain
reaching toward the sun,

touching the rays of the sun
through sky and cloud.
There was such light in his eyes.
I was afraid to look,
but his eyes said look and see.
I was like them, the people by the sea.
I heard someone say
Moses gave our people manna,
let the Rabbi give us manna.
And I remembered the story of the manna
that appeared in the morning
on the desert floor
our ancestors walking to the promised land,
the freshest of breads,
a bread of substance
that could fill hungry stomachs
and cling to weak and tired bones,
bread that nourished and became flesh.
He said he would raise us up,
that through him we would not hunger or thirst,
through him we would know God, his father,
who had sent the manna, who had sent him.
I shook with fear.

2.

I sat on rocks by the sea,
watching the calm water,
thinking of the Rabbi
away from the questioning crowd.
His eyes were so bright.
His eyes told a story
we could not hear.
I ate his presence as if it were bread.
I drank his presence as if it were wine.
But still I was afraid.

3.

I sat on rocks watching the blackening sky,
the thin line of white light and gold
above water and earth.
I heard no sound of a man walking over stone.
I heard no breath.
But there he was, standing before me,
and I was no longer afraid.

What Is Love

What is love but
the generous grace he gives,
the knowledge that all we have,
the everydayness of our lives,
is precious, even

when those we love hurt us,
and we in turn them, and we
ask to be forgiven, and we forgive them,
because that is what God does
in giving us in his love all we need.

After Su Tung-Po

I drink red wine
and talk to the moon.

Old friend, where have you been?
Why is my heart so cold?

Such light, and still I am afraid.
Such foolishness.

I pray in the moonlight.
I coax my soul from the dark.

Together we pray,
grateful for the light.

Walking at Sunset

I walk at sunset,
Past creeks, eroding banks,
The field where I startle

Two rabbits who watch my steps,
Then disappear under
Pines sweeping grass.

Nine ducklings paddle to shore.
I walk and smoke.
I wonder where you are.

At Dusk, Summer

Bright sky,
High white clouds drift by.

Birds sing,
Glide from tree to tree.

Cows amble toward barn.
I slowly walk home.

Summer Rain

Light breaks through gray sky,
Cardinal flashes red.

Oriole forages in wet dirt,
Bright against black soil.

Breeze shakes leaves,
Rain wets hair and face.

I smoke in the cool air.
No worry. No care.

Rising Mist

Mist rises through trees.
Hello again valleys,

Mountains and rivers
I've long left.

Thank you, Lord,
For this peace I've found at home.

Night Coming On

Ground wet from afternoon rain.
Birds break across gray sky.

Dark soon. I will sleep well.

Vocation

Twice you called. Twice I failed to answer.
You called first when I was a child.
Innocent, untutored, I could not hear,
Despite the love I felt for you, and so
I chose to live outside your love.
And the world corrupted me.

Crushed by the world, then renewed by your
    love,
I heard your call, but I could not give up
The life I had, the small pleasures that hint of you.
You called again, and finally I knew
That my life would have no purpose
Until I surrendered it to you.

Poem for Mary Magdalene

You, who watched the crucifixion.
You, who waited at the tomb.
You, the first at the tomb
on that glorious morning.
You, who heard his voice
and knew he was alive.

How can they think of you as temptress,
as a woman of the flesh,
as earthly lover of the one
whose love is beyond all earthbound love,
a love we know only through
his own temporary mortality?

False singers, they perfume their own hair,
anoint their own bodies
and call us, rising from the throng
of writhing bodies, reaching
toward us with jeweled hands
gleaming with false light.

Let us kneel with you at his feet.
Let us pray with you before his cross.
Let us stand with you before his tomb.
Let us hear his voice on the dusty road.
Let us know his pure light, as you did.
Let us make their words archaic.

Mother and Son

She sits in the half lit room,
eyes half closed in prayer.
Outside, it is still dark, and all

in the house but her are asleep.
She looks up as the room
fills with light, a new day

breaking, the light like none
she or anyone else has ever seen.
Whiter than snow, the light

of the angel at the tomb,
to see it would frighten most.
But she, with a light of her own,

greater than that of angels,
knows nothing of fear,
knows only this light of purest love.

Among the Fallen Leaves

I have no desire to be
The one with answers,
The one who can fix
All the problems of
The unfortunate

Lives of those who
Turn away from self,
The rubble within.
Instead, I want
To fix the self,

To know I am
No better than,
Perhaps even less than,
Decomposing leaves
Making good, rich soil

To hold the roots
Of the old and new
Trees growing
In this soil, just
As God has willed it.

Meditation on Lines from Psalm 86

I was near death, an empty man
With a granite heart and an icy soul.
My family had abandoned me,
So I sought comfort in the arms of shades,
Lonely women who longed like me
For moments of life in the dead land.

Poor souls, all they found with me was
    more death.
I tormented one, rejected others, failed
To the see the good in some,
The women who may have made good wives.
Still, I sought them out, their painful lives,
And together we eased our pain.

I could not save myself. How could I?
I was a child dependent on a mother
For food, a change of clothes, a roof.
Yet, I had no father, a man of character
And strength to guide me.
I was no such man myself.

I had traveled in the waste land of my culture,
And I had reached its end. There were only
Two roads left, death or life,

The choice was mine to make.
But I did not know what life was,
Until the Holy Spirit came to me as light.

I was no Paul chosen for great things.
But I was given new life and this story to tell:
That the Lord waits for each of us.
Even though we wander far from him,
He is always with us.
He patiently walks with us.

And so I sing with the psalmist,
"For great is your merciful love toward me;
You have delivered my soul from the depths
    of Sheol."

Dark Days, Light

I couldn't remember who sang it
But I remembered the title
And so in a somewhat nostalgic mood,
Perhaps for darkness, dark days of youth,

When I was lost like Dante without a Virgil
To guide, or a Beatrice to intercede,
I went in search of the song,
Found it and was taken back

More than thirty years to a year of suffering
When I truly thought I might end up
Sitting like a crow on Massachusetts Avenue, broken
Lonely, drinking the wine of death,

Fighting the demons of the past, fighting you.
I wanted to smash my face against a wall,
Not a fist, my face, I wanted to bleed,
And in my foolish romantic view

I walked in the rain on Massachusetts Avenue,
Just another dead soul lost in pain.
Although I love another who loves me,
If you die before I do

I will leave roses on your grave.
Despite the pain you caused me,
    the pain I caused you,
I will pray, as I do each day, for you
That you never know darkness, only light.

"Jesus, I don't want to die alone"

It's Lent, and I hear it again,
that song filled with the pain and sorrow
of every human being on earth
who has ever lost his way or has believed
there was no one or nothing to turn to,
that there was something you wanted,
you couldn't say what it was,
that there was no comfort,
who has lived through times
when songs like this only make it worse.
My heart doesn't ache, it bleeds
as I sit listening to Johnny Cash,
drinking tea, watching
the lost souls of Providence pass by,
and for a moment it is the seventies again
and I am with them, wandering.
We weren't going to get married.
I wasn't going to get that job.
That book would never get written.
I would always wander these streets
on cold February nights,
the dark sky full of the threat of snow,
flames tormenting my heart,
the loss of the woman I loved.
My heart is bleeding, but today it bleeds prayer
for the people outside,

for the wife who sits beside me
drinking her own cup of tea,
for the family miles down the road,
and the friends back home,
for all those I have loved,
and those I have hurt,
for all who have asked for my prayers,
for the God who never abandoned me,
who sits with me now,
whose son died for me and for all of us,
who never lets anyone who loves him die alone.

First Snow of Winter,
Thinking of a Poem by Ryōkan

The first snow of winter begins just past eleven.
You can hardly see it at first, nothing sticks,
but it glimmers in the light of the night
and leaves small beads on my coat.
I am like a child again, ready to play,
ready to miss a day of work.
I am again the young student
who would stay up all night reading and smoking,
sipping tea or brandy, watching the snow,
wrapping himself up in the silence.

I drink tea, pray the hours,
consider sitting outside to smoke my pipe,
but I set the alarm and go to sleep.
When I wake, the ground is covered,
    the street clear.
There'll be work today, but I am filled with joy.
No one is up, no cars speed by, no barking dogs.
Just the silence and the night sky,
the light of the new snow.
Once again I remember how good everything is.
The sorrow has lifted.

Watching and Listening to Birds at Belmont Abbey as the Sun Sets

—after James Wright

At first they look like dark leaves
Unfurled on the just budding trees,
But when you look closely you see birds
Gathered on the branches, perched
In the last light of the day
As the bells call the monks to prayer.
From this distance you can't tell the mix of bird,
Blackbirds, perhaps, since they shine black
   in the sun,
And on the lower branches
You make out a flash of red among the black,
While below you see a flash of blue and white.
All around you the birds sing and chatter.
Watch and listen. There is so much to learn.

END

ACKNOWLEDGEMENTS

New Poems
Suddenly, "Art in Motion," Charlotte Area Transit System, the Arts and Science Council of Charlotte-Mecklenburg and the Light Factory; Lilacs in Bloom, *Agora*; Mother and Son, *Review for Religious: A Journal of Catholic Spirituality*; Meditation on Lines from Psalm 86, *Pilgrim: A Journal of Catholic Experience*

The Hungry Walker, Volcanic Ash Books, 2001
Listening to Music, Watching Gray Sky, *Oyster Boy Review*; Stones, *Agora*; After Rain, *WOL: Writer-On-Line.com*

Wherever, Cincinnati Writer's Project, 1999
Starlings Gather, Morning, *ELF: Eclectic Literary Forum*; Pain, *Rendezvous*; Far, *Ethos* (Idaho State University); After My Father's Death, *ELF: Eclectic Literary Forum*; April Night, Eclipse, *The Distillery: Artistic Spirits of the South*; To Think of Akira Kurosawa's *Dreams* One Morning Driving to Work, *Gargoyle*; Prayer, *Ant Farm*, and Michael J. Bugeja, *The Art and Craft of Poetry* (Cincinnati: Writer's Digest Books), 1994; Reading Jotei, *ELF: Eclectic Literary Forum*; Reading Lu Yu, *ELF:*

Eclectic Literary Forum; Tea, *Rendezvous*; Wherever, *Yawp*

The Tools of Ignorance, Cincinnati Writer's Project, 1997

To Have Knowledge, *OntheBus*; God Explains Earth to His Angels, *Calapooya Collage*, and Michael J. Bugeja, *The Art and Craft of Poetry* (Cincinnati: Writer's Digest Books), 1994; A Bagful of Fish, *Spectrum*; Near Henry's Lake, in August, *Crazy River*; Grasshoppers, Summer, *The Warrior Poet*; Vulture, *Snowy Egret*; Birds, *Snowy Egret*; Leaf, *Readings from the Midwest Poetry Festival*

About Water, Dry Crik Press, 1993

The Earth Does Not Need Us, *Turning Wheel: Journal of the Buddhist Peace Fellowship*; When Evening Comes, Winter, *Turning Wheel: Journal of the Buddhist Peace Fellowship*; Marsh, Martha A. Strawn, *Alligators: Prehistoric Presence in the American Landscape* (Baltimore: Johns Hopkins UP 1997); Houses, Winter Morning, *Big Scream*; Farm, *The Antigonish Review*; Field, *Big Scream*; Field, Late Winter, *Big Scream*

Quotations from Scripture are from the Revised Standard Version Bible, Second Catholic Edition, Ignatius Press

ABOUT THE AUTHOR

Kevin Bezner was born in Maryland in 1953 to Alfred Francis Bezner, a U.S. Navy sailor, and Mary Rita Sullivan, a telephone operator. Before the age of ten, he lived in Hawaii, New York, Pennsylvania, and Virginia. The family settled in Massachusetts, his mother's home state, in 1963.

Bezner was raised Catholic and attended Catholic schools through high school, but like many young men and women seduced by secularism he left the Catholic Church while in college during the 1970s. As the years passed, he moved from agnosticism to a vitriolic anti-Catholicism and atheism. In the 1980s, Bezner's study and writing of poetry led him to Zen Buddhism, which he informally practiced through the 1990s. As a poet, he sought to know the natural world and to erase his sense of self in the practice of his art, like the Chinese and Japanese poets and artists he admired. In nature and in the writing of poetry, he felt a presence that brought him peace and calm. He explained the presence as nothing more than the result of his attentiveness to the natural world, but in his heart he knew it was something more.

On a gray March afternoon in 1998, driving through the mountains of North Carolina, Bezner experienced the presence as a brilliant light that he knew was God. Immediately, a hardened atheist was transformed into a believer in Jesus Christ with the knowledge that the Catholic Church is the one true Church. He also recognized that this was the light that had been calling him in nature and in the writing of his poetry. Four years later, after thirty years of living outside the Catholic Church, he attended Mass for the first time on Easter morning 2002. By the end of that year, he began attending Mass regularly. By 2003, he was committed to knowing fully and living by the authentic teachings of the Catholic Church.

Bezner earned a doctorate in English from Ohio University in 1991; master's degrees in English, 1989, and American Studies, 1976, from the University of Maryland; and a bachelor's in American Studies from Roger Williams in 1975. He also earned a certificate in spiritual direction from the Center for Spirituality and Ministry at Sacred Heart University in 2008; an advanced catechist certificate from Catholic Distance University in 2010; and a certificate in lay ministry from the Catholic Diocese of Charlotte in 2012. He was awarded a master's in theology, with a concentration in Sacred Scripture, from Holy Apostles College and Seminary, in 2014. Also in 2014, Bezner was ordained as a deacon in the Ukrainian Catholic Church.

Bezner has published six previous collections of poetry, edited two books on American poets, and published numerous interviews with American poets and fiction writers. His articles on the Catholic faith have been published in *Lay Witness, New Oxford Review,* and *The Catholic Thing.* He is a member of Catholics United for the Faith and the Fellowship of Catholic Scholars. He has taught literature and writing at the University of Montana, Idaho State University, Belmont Abbey College, and other colleges and universities.

●　●　○